Don Quixote
in America

Also by Sam Kashner

Poetry

Driving at Night
No More Mr. Nice Guy

Non-Fiction

A Talent for Genius: The Life and Times of Oscar Levant
(with Nancy Schoenberger)

Hollywood Kryptonite: The Bulldog, The Lady, and the
Death of Superman
(with Nancy Schoenberger)

Don Quixote
in America

SAM KASHNER

Hanging Loose Press
Brooklyn, New York

Published by Hanging Loose Press, 231 Wyckoff Street, Brooklyn, New York 11217. All rights reserved. No part of this book may be reproduced without the publisher's written permission, except for brief quotations in reviews.

Printed in the United States of America
10 9 8 7 6 5 4 3 2 1

Acknowledgments: Some of these poems have been published in the following magazines: *Hanging Loose, Harvard Magazine, Mudfish, oblek, Salamander, Talisman, The William and Mary Review* and *Verse.*

Hanging Loose Press wishes to thank the Literature Programs of the National Endowment for the Arts and the New York State Council on the Arts for grants in support of this book's publication.

Cover art by Kurt Wubbles
Cover design by Caroline Drabik

Library of Congress Cataloging-in-Publication Data

Kashner, Sam.
    Don Quixote in America / Sam Kashner.
       p.   cm.
    ISBN 1-882413-39-3 (cloth). -- ISBN 1-882413-40-7 (pbk. :
alk. paper)
    I. Title.
    PS3561.A697D66   1997
    811'.54--dc21   97-1623
                                    CIP

 Produced at The Print Center, Inc., 225 Varick St., New York, NY 10014, a non-profit facility for literary and arts-related publications. (212) 206-8465

Contents

FLO

Gogol's Soul

for Nancy Jane

blank

Swimming Lessons

Swimming Lessons

Yes, the sea has its own reasons.
It will not punish us but responds
to our pleading by repeating our names
and the names of those who fell from their
deck chairs onto the edge of the world,
those who sit in judgment at the harbor,
who greet the steamers groaning on the dark water.
It is my memory of the sea you love
and not the breaststroke I learned as a boy.
Everyone has forgotten how I fought the water,
how I wept and trembled at a stranger's words —
who tore me from my book and while the sun slept
made me float on the tired lip of the sea.

All the Great Shibboleths Are Dead

I wonder what wonderful little inn or hotel
we won't be going to this week.
Queen Esther's holiday has left a sheet to settle itself
on Dezingdorf Street so full of glass
there is no time for reflection.

Nancy has left in her car like a bride.
She is afraid to be alone with me,
my head a cloud in Vaseline.
My thoughts slip out and stare at her,
the empty chair a portrait of her boredom
or a brush stuck to her thigh.

"Everybody was my friend but I wasn't in love
with nobody," said Princess Hoenlohoe who was
really an ex-showgirl named Honeychilde Wilder.
"21" must be in mourning.
In Fantin Latour's painting Arthur Rimbaud's
wrist is a flower and his gaze pains us
as we eat our grapes bitterly in our empty bed.

And the exterminator is on his way
from Hampton to wipe out an entire colony
of carpenter ants who are now even as we speak
defiant and building a subject for us
to talk about over our dinner,
the one where we will bury the hatchet
leaving us happier than we were before.
At least before that last leaf,
still green, fell arguably from the
tree of our mutual shame.

Voyage

In the beginning you were a stranger.
I noticed your hat.   The lice came through it
and your hair was combed out in the schoolyard
where fate under its ironworks, is shaped
like a canopy for the heart's bed.
What fails is the bird and not the paradise.

For how colloquial are the stars when we see them
rub up against the side of such a boat
as our stillness?   Spinoza
and a beautiful woman walk through the plaza
of my heart, as if a dream was born there
every fortnight, and my ribs fought back
the one dizzying tear you could wring from it.

Oh I would rather be a guest than a ghost
and follow you home to the mountains
that flood your verse,
instead of being blamed for the lack of flowers
and the surfeit of bad teeth.   Your lovers voyage to you
and return alone.   We know this
because we see them weak as clouds,
their scruples a crowded prison, their brains
spilling thoughts of you like tin cups
being dragged along the bars.

Appointment at the Louvre

Once there it's hard to leave
the portrait of Cleopatra polishing her birthmark
or the statue of Hercules fighting bull-shaped
Achelous.   I can see the beauties of another time,
their flesh like tapers dripping round
targets which Cupid's arrow will not miss.

We agree to meet under the drawing of a mis-
anthrope.   This confuses you and so you leave,
storming past the Chariot of the Virgin, her round
face and hands a loathsome image to Saint Mark.
In a room devoted to keeping time,
I see the gold hours hammered into shape:

a clock from the court at Versailles shaped
like one of King Louis's mistresses —
Madame Pompadour perhaps, who spent her time
watching her lovers pile up like leaves
outside her window (a Viscount once left his mark —
a trace of powder — on the door to her theater-in-the-round).

Maybe you've gone to look at the merry-go-round
where a dozen horses in full stride, their perfect shapes
marred by poles pumping through their manes, mark
the spot where some pale Miss
Little could always leave
her starched Nurse immersed in *Search For Lost Time.*

The guards have announced it's closing time
and you have vanished into the round
world without so much as a by-your-leave.
Can I describe you to a stranger?   The shape
of your mouth, your hair dismissed
under a hat, your dress the color of Deutsche marks?

Will they ask me if you're an easy mark
for kidnappers, or if it's like you to have no idea of time?
It's simple enough, she missed
her train, the gendarme will explain in his round-
about way while your picture takes shape
in the police artist's sketchpad, its leaves

filled with the marked faces of the missing, around
                    which an untimely shape
is hovering, a foreigner's grave covered with leaves.

Blind Date

Under the clouds the nameless shoots
are cooled and our bodies blessed
with surfaces brought back
envious of our gaze.   I get jumpy
having to run the gauntlet,
putting out fires that burn the trunks
of deciduous trees.   Your presence
is a reminder of the shadows
that run like sewer pipe
under the doll houses.
But the wind is not so great
that you should feel dissatisfied
with your position, while the Wife
of Bath's milk runs under the door
and down the steps, melancholy
as the snow of cities piling up
at the edge of your bed.
The peacemakers are stalled
in traffic, but I am on my feet,
crawling back historically
to share it with you.

The Roses of Nice

At last the faint trace of a garden appears
beneath my own mysteriousness
engendered by the love you discarded like a bed.
Despite the fact that you are not here
and that the coffee is pouring like a waterfall
but is cold, I cannot accept the idea
of the unobservable mind, empty as a chair
pushed up against the door of your cabin —
so calm it could be a photograph of you
running towards the meteorite
embedded in the wall of Our Lady of Rapture.

Strumbling through life without my spinach
or the roses of Nice, I need your help
now that we are waiting for you
and the sea is filling up with rice.

You have been gone a long time
but I have not made a brother of you,
or a sister with her Chinese dolls
and allergies born of the vanishing streets
where we buried the kissing fish
and held back the crowd
like a fountain where nothing grows.

Autumn

I remember the stag
that stood outside your window
his heart pounding like a troubadour's.
But I cannot remember the ease
with which he vanished.
I remember the moonlight leaving
a kind of racing stripe
on his side.
I remember thinking
what courage it takes to be alone,
to disappear with your thoughts
into the ancient streets
where men are often mistaken
for cobblestones or newspapers.
I remember one man who wrapped
his head in a headline,
"Man Eaten By Dog He Loved."
But today the most important
thing about you is how old you are,
twenty-nine and counting.
I do remember your hair,
black as a waterfall that stops suddenly.
How unhealthy my memory is,
especially of beautiful things.
My tendency to reminisce, while admirable,
is like a blot on the landscape.
My brain, that soggy cow,
just sits in the middle of my head
bleating out your name
and insists I remember you,
your shoulder blade turning
and cutting the air.
I am in love with the stress
of everyday living.
Traffic jams and wrong numbers
leave me breathless.
When I am inconvenienced
I am incapable of sorrow.

But wait, you, my precious vowel,
my *Deus ex machina,*
you take with you into this poem
the feeling that we have come
to the end of our rope.
But this simply isn't true.
Ideas suffer like beautiful flowers
torn from their roots
by insurance salesmen, who alone
know the true value of our deaths.
I can remember you cutting onions and crying,
burning yourself for our dinner,
wearing a red shirt and relaxing,
cooking eel in a skinny pan.
Behind you stood the Con Ed building,
its blue tower glowing red in autumn
like our hearts,
that other temperamental utility
awash in flame.

The Donny and Marie Lunchbox

The Donny and Marie lunchbox is a big hit.
Every afternoon thousands of kids
are opening up Donny and Marie's heads
and pulling out tunafish sandwiches
peanut butter and jelly or cold meatloaf.
The thermos that fits in
beside the sandwich
has an action scene on it
from the Donny and Marie Show.
Donny is dancing in a white jumpsuit
with fringe on it
while Marie, teeth glowing,
sings through her hair.

Screw off the top of the thermos
and it becomes a cup
into which the kids pour their milk or orange juice.
The inside of the lunchbox
is grey and uninteresting.
It doesn't have the excitement or
beautiful costumes of Donny and Marie.
It is the other side of the klieg lights.

I wonder if Donny and Marie
take a Charlie's Angels lunchbox
to the studio with them
when they are taping a new show.
Probably not.
They probably have lunch served to them in their
air-conditioned trailers.
Or Marie skips lunch completely because
she's watching her weight
and Donny too except he won't tell anybody
because they'll think he's vain or a sissy.

Actually I would like to come into their trailers
while they are sleeping
and chop them into little pieces
and put all the pieces into
a plain black lunchbox
and take it to work with me.
Then when I am sitting up on a steel beam
of the twenty-eighth floor of an unfinished
apartment house
and the guys ask me "Hey, Sam, what've you got in there?"
I'll be able to tell them
"D&M on toast, want a bite?"

Uncle's Pipes

How sad we threw them away —
the Turkish Block,
its gleaming gooseneck:
Good for thinking he would say,
or the Church Warden we tossed out,
oblivious to its deep bowl
and long stem like a tulip —
the state flower of his tiny rooms.
I remember the hand carved
Meerschaums — a matched set —
shaped like a spouting fish,
never moved from their place
of honor among the books
(I found a dirty magazine there once)
and records — 78s mostly,
heavy as dinner plates.
During our winter visits he played
"Che Gelida Manina" from *La Boheme* on the hi-fi.
The speakers, long removed by tinkering
from their frames,
looked like horns of plenty
crackling never far from his ears.
In college, it was the Root Briar
I admired most
because it was like Duchamp's.
He married late, his wife hated smoke,
but I could see the Peterson Irish
sticking up like a periscope
from his breast pocket.
We have his favorite chair in our house.
The armrests are darkened by smoke rings
and the elbows of a man
pulling in his net.

Burial of the Combs
(A Pantoum)

To the work and good health of John Yau

Misconceptions ache to offer us a life
beyond the romance of these vague maps.
Unlike boredom empty treasures endure
within a city whose heart is a fog.

Beyond the romance of these vague maps
true pleasure never arrives.
Within a city whose heart is a fog
the mere presence of strangers summons us like a muezzin.

True pleasure never arrives.
In columns of light we preserve the sweet hours.
The mere presence of strangers summons us like a muezzin
below the margins of clouds.

In columns of light we preserve the sweet hours.
The sun grows larger in a dusty room
below the margin of clouds.
Love is fond of absolutes.

The sun grows larger in a dusty room.
Mother's combs are buried in the garden.
Love is fond of absolutes
so this time recovery is slow.

Mother's combs are buried in the garden
where geraniums pull down the sun
so this time recovery is slow
and not because the snow is falling.

Where geraniums pull down the sun
misconceptions ache to offer us a life
and not because the snow is falling.
Unlike boredom empty treasures endure.

How Often He Thought

By twilight everything that was sleeping
had changed into something that was leaving,
even the leaves in the shape of arrowheads.

We summon our uneasy tears like the fire brigade
its buckets.   Now we drift between the trees where
once we gamboled in our masks.

How terrible to lack courage! Like the sun, the sky rises
and shifts.   Mother, you arranged my life, but it is not
the miracle you waited for.   Even resemblance is mere

cupidity, a way to make the waves speak.
You filled their shape with your voice
which after all, cannot speak to me

if you fire it or send it packing, smashed by you
into an instrument of your life without
the judgment that kept us still.

Do not weep over the onion's skin
or the shower of nettles that rests in your hair.
You don't need to apologize for your sense of ballast.

Like the fresh-cut flowers, you are proud of your race.
The mistake here is in prose and not in your heart,
which is torn and worthy of our unbearable love.

An Old Puzzle

This morning our grapes are not wrathlike
but wraithlike in their Polish bowl
the size of Kosciusko's head.
(His victory I've never seen
but read about so often
I was blind with envy for their cause.)

As a boy I did stand up to Mother
but her sadness took me by surprise,
even in photographs with her hair
like a baseball diamond under lights.
Stuck in the veldt, she practices
her lullabies on another.
I don't resent him for coming
into this cagy world, a boy —
my sister named him Jonah
for the one who lost his faith.

I screwed up their idea of perfection
but sons do that, burning down their house
of baseball cards.   We distract each other.
It is in the nature of families to drift
alone in our pleasure boats
like clouds across purposeful mountains —
great as some music is when purged from the ears.

There were no stallions
or pears waiting for me
against the distance that now
cannot be seen.   The abandoned house
still has my things in it.
When I am young, everything else
finds itself settling in at last,
like the independence of our thoughts
from the rain that calls me back
to my room where your picture symbolizes
the infirmities of all things
not conquered by our breath.

As A Bee Leaves The Flower

As a bee leaves the flower
so we depart
with our arms outstretched
before blind winter
where we first spoke
in our youth, the tenderness
of our thoughts
forgiven and reemerged
in the way that a flame
is seen or avenged.
My sister remembers me
in a house filled
with leaves.   Her voice
disdains the cast
made for her foot.
The vases are empty
and filled with light.
They disturbed the
window, its shadow
shattered in a weak
moment by a man
walking home.
The street leads us
to the ocean where
the waves appear
in our cufflinks for hours.
We acclaim these ships
that bathe in this
troubled air.
The slumbering giant consults
his mythological dictionary
and takes our part
like a bird picking seeds
out of the earth,
and then he falls asleep
upon a wine-stained sleeve.

Don Quixote in America

Reading Hesiod

We are received into the land where
scales measure the sobbing lyre, the shame
of numbers pouring into the sea.
The terrible past is built within the air
that sinks thoughtlessly into the
painting we inhabit.
Or is it the closer we are
the more alert to our love?
But this too goes unpunished.
Reading Hesiod is a precaution we take
when we are seldom home, or perhaps
unsure of our footing when coming
out of the movie theater in winter,
smelling of light and wasting
all that quiet.

This World

Ancient world, your new world is ready.
The shadows of birds move along the road.
There is a young girl on the road,
her hair wet and slick as a head of lettuce.
People say she lives in the shadow of her mother.

The farmers pull down the scarecrow
and carry him off like a worker
who collapsed in the field.

In town, the John Deere salesmen
stare out of the showroom window
at a roe tied to the hood of a car.

These scenes are not real
but shards of glass
that fall through the sky at night.

I am lifted out of the sea
to which I have been anchored —
its glittering heart groaning with freighters.

Saint Simon stands on his pillar,
his heart becoming a figure of speech.

My reflection wavers in the mirror.
It reminds me of this life which I place
beside you like a copy of *The Persian Letters*.

Aesop's Master

A clock strikes ten in the distance,
and a good thing too.
The old actor's face
lights up with malice.
"Oh, youth"
as the saying goes,
"thank you for reminding me
of your age."
Xanthus, Aesop's master,
returns to us with his hands
held out like a beggar's.
The door handles are all broken.
The portfolios have been
torn from their leather
cases and scattered
along the windy streets.
I become absorbed in the task
of gathering them up:
drawings of pillars recall
the Temple of Diana, which an unknown
artist, out of his profound
boredom, brought into being
because the rent was due.

Portrait of Orpheus as a Young Horticulturist

Orpheus is digging a hole in our garden.
The light is his shovel,
the light that leans against the fence
like a cowboy picking his teeth.
I suppose Eurydice's flowers
are the ones beside the great hole he is digging.
The branches are covering his head.
They are pointing the way.

He is building a mountain range
so that he might sink deeper into the earth.
He is looking for a way back,
to join the dead in their awakening,
to bring her as you would
a valuable witness
back to her own flowers.
She must be protected
from the leaves that fall
here heavy as stones.

There is a boat waiting for him
under the earth
and a tunnel empty as a sleeve
and white as the paper hat
he must wear when entering
the city where she is waiting for him
in a yellow dress,
waiting to be carried up
the long rope of flowers
she has left for him.

She is whispering something
between the spaces of earth no one can see.
She is asking him for the time
but to save her from the fate of all flowers
he must be rude.
He must not turn as if to say
"what is it love can refuse?"

Or else the world that waits for him like a bed
will remain empty and blind as a star.

The Helmsman Invites the Waves to Speak

The drowned enter us
like Palinurus who entered the sea,
his breath unraveling
under an iron sky.
His hands slipped from the wheel
that was his terrible job.
Without a word he fell,
unmarried, into the roaring ear of his fate.

We have come through a crack in the wall,
our beginning ended here.
Exhausted by the silence of a woman
lost under a huge veil,
the sun drops its sealing wax
onto the veins of men.

Deep-sea divers
handcuff us to the trees.
We can see death's sail moving over the earth.
Smoke from the asylum blows over the darkening fields.
The shore is insistent.
A faint star will grant you your last wish,
the windows burning in the widow's dream.

The day of your birth
was a day of restitution,
as in the birth of a star — no longer possible.
Weary, even in the sun where we live,
beardless as a nocturne
and brief as air.

This love which is a mask
follows us and is cruel to the idea
that a single word is your undoing
(a wish is like that only more so).
The agonies of the dark
bring us to your table radiant with bread.
We sleep but do not dream.
The body is an earring to a god
who sits propped up among broken ships,
a phantom drawn from life.

Aquacade

Our neighbors, desirous of rain,
confront the sea at night.
Their pain is elastic and stretches
through dreams and into the throats
of the singers of old songs,
whose pockets are deep with dust.
The sad discomfiture of the plumber
as he bends over a small body of water
is different from the sailor's,
who hears the terrible cape of the wind
sweep over him.

It was you, impalpable ocean, with your distance
and solitude that kept us apart —
your great balconies, which are always crumbling,
your statues, which appear in the foam
and disappear in nameless gulfs. It was you,
enemy of oars, who broke off our engagement by
    throwing a net
over the possibility of a better life.
It was you who dislodged the tables in the stateroom
and sent them floating like a chain of islands,
free of the actual weight of the world.

Through the great hollows of ships
you wander, full of questions that must go
unanswered.   Each port of call brings an inexplicable
word to your lips: the name of an ancient ancestor,
a pirate singing a European song, or a sailor
polishing the impossibly small universe
of the porthole in the middle of the night.

All of this confusion has left me
speechless beside your tremulous waters.
The sails block out the sun
which has been rising somewhere.
Without it, no one will see you arrive.
Your own voice will fall silent
like the sea at night.
Everything visible will start to withdraw from you.
But do not worry about the horizons —
they are simply the petals of some futuristic
flower, which will not open until you are safely home.

At the Plinth

The sailboats, crestfallen, now drift
past the finish line where the gentian-
colored sky sends back its most urgent message:
"Awake, obsequious painters and recumbent weathermen.
Remember, your assiduousness is not unlike my own."
With this the great bells stop ringing
and the sun in its silo of clouds admonishes us.
Only our wisdom descends stupefied like a magpie
before the hour of our death at sea.

The stars immutable and hunted by telescopes
tell us nothing of our lives —
a portrait variegated and bucolic,
we see it with our eyes closed.
The earth rises up without wings,
its rivers exuberant yet confused.
We wail on these rivers and wait.

Our hands hold up a book about the Erie Canal.
Too much light makes it impossible to read;
even the pages are too cold.
Leaning over the side of the boat
I see the "call letters" that distinguish us
from the other travelers.
What is left for those who move between them,
pulled by elaborate eddies and erased by fog,
our great lights adumbrating the shore?

Don Quixote In America

To the Eden Rock!
Where the wind is clamoring
over the empty trails.
The mountains have no way to greet you
and they are irreplaceably content.
The birds, strategic and gallant
in their superannuated nests,
are not the most ambitious of nature's outcasts.
The stars, like some demented medicine
cabinet, lie ruined on the shore.
It is embarrassing to get
such a tongue-lashing from you, Sancho Panza,
years after the flies
have been chased away from your collar bone —
and the thunder like the music of recognition
or the tenderness of the body has faltered.
I am not afraid of Narcissus,
his heart like a sieve,
his mouth drawn in outline
red as the blood of a frontier town.
I was alone in that place he kept
where the tawny edge is lifted
like a window dreaming of the sea —
with the moon moaning in a tender
and forgettable breath "good morning, dear."
The park approaches its destiny
without feeling endangered
or left with nothing to talk about but the wind.
Together we blame the violet flowers
for letting us fall —
for everything that happens, even the haircut
which was just so much structural wailing —
but tonight it is safety last
and the heart is deliberately silent.

Hero Afraid of Water

Pink buds are wandering like sewage,
rusty fragments of the sea
rejected like a lover whose cholera is a kiss.
As the long day approaches, its solitude
so literate and unambiguous,
you even stop talking to yourself for a change.

The deer on the other side of the fence
nibble on the moon-stained leaf.
With a drop of water we fill our cups,
circling the bridge like a storm
pretending to suffer from some tropical depression.

The aloe vera will keep us busy
as it mocks our long vigil at the sun's mirror.
There is no death without enclosure.
No enclosure without the expanse of the waves.
And no waves without the bathers
to nurse us back to health.

Hero, afraid of the water, watches us
like a lifeguard without limbs
setting fire to her couch
with a match between her teeth.

How often must we recoil from the towels
we put between ourselves and the sea
and how much oil slips through fingers
and the burning skin that comes off
in the ancient theater of the shower?
Nature is repetition
and so we rub our eyes like a boxer
waking up to his own stars.
Our fists like two mountains
couldn't be closer than the tide,
that wicked accident of the moon.

The worst thing you imagine does not occur.
Other things sit for their portrait
in the mind's eye: the conquistador
dead on the beach, his helmet a horseshoe crab
half-buried in the sand, his teeth ground
into flour the twins scoop up in their pails.

Revenge Of The Nereids

Why do you wear such a long face, Andromeda?
You who come from a race of soldiers
and are the direct descendant of a bathing beauty?
The moon towers over the tallest girl
even in the treehouse
where we go to make fun of the boys.
Still, even from there we cannot touch
its cold face lit from within
by the mother of a great star.

You make me jealous
leaving our bed like a man
running back to his wife.
The stains on our sheets
are like the tiny islands on a map.
The cartographers will use them
to reach us; otherwise your other lovers
might find us wanting.

There is a blue light in the trees
but no shadows.
All the husbands are gone.
We remember the reason for their absence
is a beautiful woman,
one whom we too would love,
if we only had the chance.

A nightgown can become a shroud
if there is no one around to remove it.
Our men might own the sea
but they pay a terrible price
for Poseidon's sceptre,
Their women finding safe harbor
in each other's arms.

From that moment on all their victories
are as wasted as the wine
running down a drunkard's chin.
Or, as one of my sweethearts put it —
empty as our own miserable nests
the ones built atop the pubic bone.
Tonight, Andromeda wears her veil.
But I remember how beautiful she looked
in her empty house.

Daughter to so much suffering,
we follow you on this path
with its broken blossoms, the sad air
the sheepish clouds
white as Helen in her chair
the unjealous bride
wearing out her welcome on the empty lawn.

I used to listen to her
with my head cocked to the side
like a dog watching its mistress
stealing a kiss.
I worshipped her like a poet worships the sea.
But she kept retreating.
Now, I have to put my thoughts of her
together like a constellation
in order to see her again
stretching out on a new bed,
calling out to me like an echo,
her hair the color of flame
illuminating my path.

The Recruit

During the Crimean War, it was not an uncommon sight
for soldiers to see gatherings of well-dressed spectators
picnicking above the battlefield.

Every day they come to watch us —
coiled up, moving in secret
formations on the grass.
The beautiful ladies
notice when we fall
how our buttons press
against the red earth like wax
hardening under a signet.
Soon torches will be set up
all over the horizon
and the missing will
bury their shadows in that light.
Within earshot
of a forbidden card game
the horses stick their heads
into buckets of rusty water
and dream of being hoisted up
into the unstabled sky.
A field mouse runs over
the dark mouths of the cannons,
quiet now, like lion-headed
fountains overrun by grass.
The only smoke is from the
officers' pipes and a fire
of twigs and useless maps.
Our scarves are hats
that keep this morning's
chill from our ears.
I clean my sight
with the stem of a leaf
and check it by taking
aim at the mountains,
their lime-colored steeples
sucked in by the clouds.

It is a woman's voice I hear
under the waves of men
coming toward us —
a girl's, really, pulling the combs
out of her hair and laughing
not at me
but at my serious ways.

Pictures of an Inhibition

Intermittence: A Love Poem

Love is always walking.
In a hundred cities its voice
is full of odors, nocturnal and witless.
Love faces itself across the great
expanse of unarbored places
with their terrible winds and the greedy sea
nowhere in sight.   But love is good company
when you see the dark brush floating before you,
its one eye in the water and the other
spouting such pieties that your heart hurts
under the weight of so many imaginary clouds.
But it is there that the starlings
have begun to haunt the shore, revolving
like love itself into a mirror of farewells.
So we descend to the uncertain entrails
of this, our marriage bed,
and wait for the world's ambiguities
to blind us.

Failure Masked as a Show, an Ostent

What can be said of this distance
when the stars pretend to be jealous of our reach?
Depressed as a child, we mount the sunny day
and see it fall.

A boy leans against the wrong tree
and disappears into his stunning brother.
He picks up theories like a handkerchief
and is driven home by the bluest of clouds.
"Sacrifice" was the word he heard most often
from the little girls and the sick friends
who mustered praise, never objecting
to the value he placed on their affection.

"In life one must have a theme" —
the airplanes fly over summer drinks
and the earth waits for their enormous shadows
like rain searching the tide for grass,
or the clarity of affection that bastes the eye.

The most serious flowers bloom
in our childhoods and in the aching bend
of the earth, its fire arranged like a decoration
seen for miles under an empty sky (a warning from
Empedocles, our confused ancestor,
that the same principles are also poised
to rise up in our hearts).

The Water Lily Is Doomed

The water lily is doomed and scattered.
Like a powder it trembles
and drinks in pond water.
Its seeds are joined in rain
that moves under clouds
dark as the roots and embers
of a nameless flame

whose heat is the chaos of history.
The scrolls unfurled in a meadow
are chaste compared to this
earthly rain that knows no distance
and conquers sleep.
Underground, the statues
and their lovers remember the
harbors, and the stars that harbored them.
The water lily lives on the surface of the water
like an eye and is repeated
around an unclean heart: It is a grave of
reflections that frees us from
the heights of its weeping.

The cities are peopled with
breathers of fire, their words
are cinders on the tongue of
a talkative man who holds
out a white glove, watching
it fall like a note in an opera.

Unidentifiable in Rain

What did I do wrong?
The autumn cherry, untied,
hidden behind the shed,
comes upon us like a thought,
determinate and tender.

The spokes of a wheel
go around our breathing.
The city air has a siren in it.
The children wake up
confused as ghosts
trampled in their clothes.

A sad nerve runs through the streets
where blueberries reflect the absent night,
which is never as feminine as air
or the giggling perspective
of what passes bitterly between travelers.
Winter fills our mood
like jars made of earth
that the earth abandons.

What matters in our village
is the threnody of moccasins and ink.
The stars groan with their unfortunate
dinginess, hanging out for everyone to see.
We discover our opposites in these postures
that cake over and break our will.

The birds hum without questions
in the air of silk, and after them
the clouds appear above the gum trees —
which is where onyx is made.

And you have won the prize
delivered out of love.   We have
saved it for you like an ending, the one
that comes along once in a lifetime.
Your profile is the face of god
who beckons us into this garden
overgrown with tears.

Sonnet

The goats have taken the garbage in with them
and we are left with everything else: your
heart a human bell, a rose without a stem,
a pump whose air is pure.
United we stand in a shallow grave,
reduced to absolute necessity,
or fast asleep in the shade
of an olive tree in Sicily.
An army pantomimes a crowd.   I hear
your voice among them like the loon
that carries your name in its plastic ear
across a styrofoam lagoon.
Your dreams occur out of sequence
in a house where all suffering begins.

Poem in Envy of Picasso's *Acrobats*

The seams of her stockings break through the mist,
the sky like a robe opened and dreaming of the earth.
A plume of suffering decorates her.

I sit here with the aspirations of a foot
turning a wheel and resist the wings
that have turned uncontrollably into hibiscus —
the kind of cruel miracle whose home is the breath of youth.

Stripped down and beaten with an armful of bracelets,
I shall never remember the bony compromises of the mob.
The fields below are laughing and burning —
their clarity is persistent, like the thick
glass that magnifies her entrance.

The dead follow us like the luminous memory
of a painting in which a river rushes out of a doorway.
Our friends have fled; haunted by their insensitivity
we remove the evening's earrings, its troubled signs.
The lovers are not yet ominous but they
are glistening.   Beyond the love of books
there is the toughness of fate.
Our thesis is the vernal ear and our nostalgia
a whisper.   Beyond the stream is a country of cuckoos,
not all of whom, as we rise from our beds,
hear us weeping, tremulous as boats in a sea of rooms.

Vehemence & Opinions

Oh empty heart,
virile as five sailors!
Accidents fertilize the rocks
that cry out
"what is left for me?"
while smoke rises from the outhouse,
or is it steam from a broken shell?
The rain stops us from growing.
A lifting of the covers
reveals a cannibal
who once marched in a procession.
Dark as an orchard they moved
toward the city hall,
their baskets swaying in the wind.
It was a storm full of mushrooms
that cannot be eaten.
We choose to leave our
garbage in the snow,
held back by a wreath of bricks,
sunlight twitching on the ground
like someone stepping into a puddle.
Life shifts and passes
with a curtain's shudder,
the heart a painted clock.

Pictures of an Inhibition

Like the pictures of a fire that peer
into the annals of a libidinous tribe
my heart is full of allegory and the rain
knows this to be true.   Oh stars, breathe on me,
the last of your subjects to learn this lesson!

The casual observer crumbles onto the bed
and is witness to the never-ending whiteness of his room.
Outside is where the mystery is:
The leaf in its nervousness.
The ruined house and its lost gaze —
unburdened as any man is from himself
in a kind of peril where no one can save you
but the axe in your hand.   Onto your shoulders
a blouse falls like a bloody handkerchief.
Your blue eye is gravely walking through the grass
and gartered leg of the world into the drafty castle.

Such delicate impossibility is like a summons
from the Spanish moon to each heart —
a sign to stand pat though the tears of trees
may conk us on the head and the bland morning is insistent.
I too was once scared of the sentimentalists
but that was before you strayed into my tent
and with one gesture solved all of my problems.

How can I thank you, you who entered the air
like a boy putting on his shirt
and who almost wept at the sight of the sun
so keenly lit, the window of a house
built in Braille?

Eleven from a Bestiary

1. The Owl

Behind every great woman
There is an owl
Controlling her most basic gestures
Smoothing her feathers
And making it easy for her
To see in the dark.

2. The Dromedary

While wandering in the desert
I smoke a pack of camels
And become thirsty.
Like the dromedary I can go
For days without expressing myself.

3. The Ewe

Animal of vowels
When you were born
The stars stood at attention
Like sheep
In a faraway meadow.

4. The Cat

Roaming the bookshelves Dante's cat
Studies his master's sad expression
Kissing him on the brow
Like Beatrice in a dream of happier times.

5. Pigeons

Honorary citizens!
What do you call home —
Statues, awnings?
You own the avenues streaked with grey
You who shat upon the bus shelters
And built your nests in the neighborhood marquees.
We will always remember you
Air force of the ancient cities of man.

6. The Zebra

The Z in zebra
Hangs over our heads
Like a triangle struck once
In an orchestra.
The zebra follows its star
Swathed in bandages
And stops to drink from
A hole in the earth
Filled with dust
And its own reflection.

7. Sirens

Sirens, how long
Must I fondle your unimaginable legs
Your voices vain as sunlight?
Flirtation is the highest form
Of flattery
But must you be so obvious?

8. The Crocodile

You climb out of the swamp
And through the revolving doors
Of Henri Bendel's
Where the bargain hunters
Seal your fate
With their credit cards.

9. The Monkey

If I could I would
Make a monkey out of everyone
And send them to the top of the mountain
To beat their chests
Like dictators of banana republics.

10. The Turtle

I ride the giant turtle to the edge of the sea
Our path is a straight line
My shoelaces click against its shell
Lily pads of linoleum turn our heads.
Dreaming in slow motion
We live for a thousand years.
The turtle carries a message to my beloved
But cannot right itself.

11. The Lion

I stuck my head inside the mouth
Of Willie "The Lion" Smith
And there I saw a big red room
With a piano playing all by itself
"You're nobody till somebody loves you."

Gogol's Soul

Letter Poem to John Ashbery

I guess you could call this
a dear John letter
but not really
at least not in the
sense of jilting you
but of jealousy angling
for your ear, erudite and
hot for centuries.
For years I've heard rumors
about long walks through
Chelsea's tainted gardens —
prosy precursor to your
one hour at the keys.
I record your impressions
as if they were my own
and get dressed up
just to meet you:
standing all day
outside your place
smoking you out
by throwing Gitanes
unlit against your windowpane.

Finally, I saw you
biting off more
than you could chew.
Handing things over
to a boy wearing pince-nez
and running shoes.
Another admiring mouth to feed?
Leaning against a wall thinking
you have poems that live on
though you're childless,
in a world they did not make,
I rose up like a wave
to greet you but
a taxi took you by surprise
and you were gone.

Typewriter ribbons flew
from the tallest spires
and purple prose
spurted from our veins
the day you returned
with your copy of
Impressions d'Afrique,
passages underlined in black ink.
What is lost in you
a little boy will take back
writing in a notebook, impatient,
poring over secret maps
in a bungalow in upstate New York.

Doctor Proust

In this way we are all made ill
by the scented trees of Illiers,
including the one you and Marcel
planted when you were boys.
The reflection of a footbridge
wraps itself around the shiny
surface of a watering can.
Marcel holds it in his hand
while you dig past the round shadows,
a bed for your first patient,
this apple tree.
Above your heads, the church
spires appear to move.
It is a thought you too
will keep at the point
where two rivers meet.
One day you'll come back
to the place renamed Combray
to look for the very tree,
with its rings dark
as his eyes that were open
when he forgave her
and remembered all.

Wilde At Berneval

At Oxford you helped Ruskin build his road
and pushed a wheelbarrow into an ode
on Ravenna, city of ancient olive woods
stunted and silver like the procession of monks
in their hoods passing the Pitti Palace
where you wept in a marble room.

Back home a brilliant future loomed,
but like an angel at a banquet you sailed
to America and saw a convict reading Dante
in a tiny jail.   In Leadville, they lowered you
into the Matchless Mine, "graceful even in a bucket."
Tactless words began appearing in the press.
"Hate as eternal negation" couldn't mean less
to the boy eating finger sandwiches on your couch,
his face like a hyacinth.   After the arrest,
you sat in Oakley Street, the portrait of a palimpsest.

Gogol's Soul

Dear Gogol, how sad you are:
your temperament, shed like a tear, or
the first leaf of a sapling
skinny as Pushkin's bride.

Here in the sign painter's city,
the capitol with its domes
like golden loaves of bread,
you stick out like a nose
dislodged and transcendent.

You shiver like a cylinder
in your best blue coat.
The proud intentions of youth
are a sentry box carried off
by the wind.   It takes you
to another shore, to brood
among the Swiss chocolatiers,
whose carriages smash into
a wall of fruit.   Oddest
of all Russians, your name
sounds like someone rushing off

to walk on the wrong side of the street,
your legs a pair of scissors cutting up the air.
Mysteriously, your words escape, flooded
in the melting disapprobation of snow.
And now, in the province of solitude,
an admission — it comes from the boy
who trembled when a chest of drawers
was opened and you wept on a broken chair,
as a book was brought to ashes
and the pure obstruction of fame.

Scriabin Approaches

I dream of these tetchy clouds and weep
for our lost right arms.
We are pressed like grass
into the face of this warm night,
more hidden than we realize
at the first glimpse into our empty cups.

Your words move us along, like a walk-in closet.
Your thoughts are full of sweaters
and moccasins no one has walked in.   However,
the burden of proof lives in the trees,
the leaves sinking into the elephant's back.
Tomorrow, everyone will be on time, the bank
teller will fall to her knees and the sun
will refuse to keep its balance
thinking to itself "I have already done so much —

the brows of men are sweaty enough as it is."
You and your mother breathe over the iron railing.
The ship roars by the place you left,
so anxious to forget this is not
the end of the life you know,
but a sudden shift from the sea to the air
like a runner being raised up on the shoulders
of a beast who has been unable to scare
anyone but himself.
Sucked back into the bath
the ball of your foot holding up the wall
you will be washed in the blood of your betters
and everyone will know you as the princess
who sits behind the cascades and snorts,
your edicts purer than the love letters
handed down in the
bitterness of later years.

In Memoriam to the One Addressed as You

And I will miss him, as Dolores Del Rio
is missed by her fans —
the fir trees of Albania.
His picture is too close and crooked.
It is a portal of sorts and I look
out with schistaceous eyes at the Visigoths
delinquent and unconvinced.   Their arrival is
the arrival of the past.   It is my tribute to his
thoughtless beauty that I kill.   What collapses
when I name it, what is capable of this wicked motto?
His name insinuates itself like a symbol
bound up in the phrase "elegant but trembling,"
like Dr. Clitterhouse in a mansion the size of my blush.
For breakfast we descend with our lips pressed
against our appetite for self-consciousness.
And where did the sun go when you went out for
your walk and people disappeared behind a cloud?
It could've been the track team: approaching figures
who pierce the air with the sweetness of aspirations,
misguided as a leaf no longer aching
for its shadow to fall.

Press to Return

Tell me, what is it that listens
when you are asleep?
That passes the wheelhouse
in its humming silence?
What is the name of the ghost
that hovers like a tree hovering
above a glade?
And what does the appearance
of an erasure in the right-
hand corner of the eye
mean to the melancholy bather
with his mouth open like a fish
facing the sea?

I can taste this bitter root,
its false scent pricking
the air that walks behind me.
You have seen it, too.
But only in your deepest wanderings,
behind the house you stabbed
with your heart.
In the lovers' cave, a shadow is
moving, its young breath
stoking a fire.
The sounds of nature play
on a phonograph.
Here, Echo broke her silence.
Between two rocks, her voice
drowned without calling for help.
Now you speak with the same words —
your song of long absences.

Press to return to the beginning
of this heresy like a thunderstorm
carried from one place to another
in a swift boat.
You are the captain of this empty bell
that rings among strangers, and
reminds us, in the strictest sense,
of our ascent past the watery
houses of the dead.

The Anesthesiologist

Stands back
like the shyest wife in a harem,
all skill vanishing beneath his white veil.

It is not sleep the body is after
but disunity.
Who is the worthy man
whose heart will not let itself
sink into a fear of death?

Here both are alone
facing this eclipse
with the composure of runners
who must lie down in the grass and breathe.

You who are stretched out on the table —
you will appear at least once in every form,
a shadow whose good fortune
may not return.
You are not going crazy.
The mind of a wound is too great
to be overshadowed
by so much uncertainty.

Between you let there be nothing
as discernable as light.
The face of a man dreaming of an island
is separate from what nurtures him.
Here time is still
not what you imagined it to be.

Everything will happen to you at once.
Your thoughts will disappear.
Your breathing will blow you off course.
Therefore, to save yourself,
think of your body as a boat
waiting for the powerful fog to clear.

While you are recuperating,
the emotions will stop by to see you,
groggy, yet resting comfortably
in the arms of an infinite sorrow
that cannot be undone.

The tide rises up to greet you
even as consciousness retreats —
at that moment a choice is being made.
It is always the wrong one
but it is always right —
your strength is in waking up to this.

Redolence: An Eclogue

I didn't notice I had been dreaming of such things:
the sad hills with their newborn shadows,
a windowpane filled with the branches of distant trees,
their own sensations a thousand years old.
Horizons are so inevitable:
they are compassionate and grow larger when the words
bon voyage are said.
The faces at the strange heart of my dream
are watching me as I fold the newspaper and begin to read.

The terrible things I encounter are merely words
but the picture of luggage in an advertisement,
the invoice of some unknown life, causes me to weep
as I do in the office of human tenderness where I work
day and night, rehearsing every gesture
that we will see in the future and borrowing
the useless symbols that gather in a crowd.

The car which races by in front of the house —
its sudden fame brings such happiness
to the youngster's face!
The driver is more real to him than life itself.

What are your plans, you who live in the future?
What kind of poets will you produce
when all of China has been made conscious of itself?
My God! I would sooner give up hope
than continue to imagine this world
in which the earth and sky
are doomed to think of themselves as portholes
opened in an early dawn.

But consanguinity is not everything,
as the stolidness of the past will eventually prove.
The meat lockers are open for inspection.
There you can see your breath and behave for a moment,
unlike a basket of flowers, in a truthful way.

Romantic Notion

Love's vermilion mouth arrives to tell us
something special is waiting in the wings.
What can it be that is so hair-raising
we are afraid to kiss it on the lips —
is it a burden or merely a thing of nature
incorrigible in its solitude?

Everywhere we look love breaks its promise
bowing its head under a crimson sky.
A romantic notion turns itself into a lake
where we threaten to remove our sailor suits
and sit around looking naked and perfectly built.

It has been said love is a rowboat tossed about
     the stormy seas
but we know people lie and tell their friends
     to hurry up and bring the beach towel.
     So relax, intensity has few brains
and anyway, no one is going anywhere without
     my permission.

The world is in love with us.
Even the oceans weep when overcome with
     our gentle beauty
and just as the notebooks of great men are
filled with such idle curiosities, so are we
wedded to the idea of staying up all night,
if only to watch the sun come up
on the side of verisimilitude.

Return of the Absent Friend
(Society is a Wave)

I am not marching but standing pat
until the wind which is all about
balance anyway, removes me.
I have not been to the airfield
with its clouds removed by the howling
of a jet.   My spirit is too clumsy, my voice
a yawn made at the edge of the bed.
You yawn over the telephone.   Nostalgia
is unimaginable when we die face up
beside a jar of sand.   You mention it's
the color of blood.   We avail ourselves
of decoration and bother to notice
who is aching to see us fail.
The sky is flooded with peculiar birds,
their wings torn but familiar.
We notice them but do not complain,
quiet in our lead aprons like paintings
with no memories.
We are made in the image of a kiss,
endless as the simple wisdom of the future.

Thanks for the Threnody

for Tom

The day is eager and passes like a child's
handwriting into some endless book where
every attempt to escape is recorded like the transcription
of a symphony; what forces itself into the ear,
a whisper, the demands of a shadow on a leaf that knows
the purity of water, the immense forgetfulness of clouds.

I cannot forgive your absence, the athleticism
of your notes pinned to the rubber tree,
the expression of myrtle, the blood upon the spyglass.
In Barhamsville, the young men sit on the stoop
and drink in the peculiar light that falls
into their eyes, fashion plates all full of food.
Feeling blessed under the awning of that much hair,
you were the ambassador of our recalcitrance,
the same one who teaches us to be on time
when combing the grounds for mint, the cold
glasses blocking our path.

In the shade I look for you, in the alleys of this
newly mown field, where one day the most dangerous
prisoners will crouch and take from you this rapture.
The young tire you out but then rescue you
in your clothes before the swans of self-consciousness
return and you fall into the sea.

Foucault is calling to you like a cuckoo bird
or an owl settling itself on the roof,
lining up, with a thread of spit, the distance
between you and the lovers who have leaped up
like Venus from her bath:
the wood now slick as the world when it was
a mess of flowers, and the tears of opprobrium
were as unknown as your own darkness.

On Her Reticence

Why leave in haste?
The beautiful dreamers have all
been broken on the wheel.

A seat in the theatre of ideas
is nothing compared to her beauty

to the striking grace with which
she leans out to touch whatever it is
that moves away when you touch it.

There is too much sun and earth, and
the choirs in their uniform poignancy
only darken the stairs.

Come out from behind the green curtains!
Your jealousy is like a famous name
for chocolate or an aria perched on the
seared mantle of a world still
reeling from the beauty of women.

Do not underestimate the sadness
of shirts no longer worn,
pleasure which has forgotten its face.

The Grand Palace with its meaning is cursed,
as if one's friends were staying simply
for dinner instead of their various reasons —
which are full of twinges of regret

like a cigarette searching for a window,
ready like anyone to declare its love.

Epithalamium

After Robert Desnos

You disappear in the flames of an hour.
A cuckoo with its tired wings
passes over you in sleep.
You waited for the Perseids
but they did not come,
a glittering fleece
blowing among the trees.
Affectionate are the cries of the monster
at the moon circling your wrist.
The end of the clouds can be seen
from your bedroom window.
It is a dream we are facing
and in which we live
without boundaries or flowers.
Behind the windowpane
a storm is waking.
There is a hole in the middle
of the storm where everything is still,
like the hole in a guitar.
There is no turning back.
The thought of you blacks out the sun.
Everything we have is buried in the world.
The chains are broken as we await the hour
that will separate us.

Hymn to Restlessness

When the last sun has gone out of the world —
no longer there to guide
the strolling lovers and lost dogs —
I will listen for your voice,
its words already fading in my ear.

The world has spread itself out before you.
With a trembling hand
it leads you through the empty streets —
streets whose cruel monuments
are unmasked by time.
You stand before these burnt columns,
your wedding dress trailing in the dirt.

Every second of your life is a mystery
complete with an unsolved crime.
You appear for a moment
bathing in the river
with the scales of a mermaid
still shimmering on your beach towel.
At the right hour the clock will strike
and you will forget how bored you were
sleeping under the stars —
dim lights of the earth's old age.

Grave diggers make your bed
and throw their cigarette butts
into the freshly dug hole.
I adore you despite the fact
that you are not here.

Please remember me
when the walls are built
above the ancient city
and the bridges collapse in a sigh.
Remember me when the sea itself changes shape
and the wind carries your voice
returning through distant reeds.